Saturn and her moons

A collection of poems by Hafsa Khokhar

Edited by Saviya Kashif

Disclaimer

This collection contains themes of grief, depression, intrusive thoughts, and emotional distress. Some poems explore dark and sensitive experiences, including references to self-harm, existential questioning, and inner turmoil.

This book is intended for mature readers (13+). Reader discretion is advised.

If you are struggling or find any of the content overwhelming, please consider reaching out to a trusted person or a mental health professional. You are not alone, and support is always available.

For those who dug me out of my grave...
...and for the one who built his home in me

For my mother, Zahida, my father, Sadiq,
and my husband, Shadman
my tether to life when the world let go of me.

"We don't read and write poetry because it's cute. We read and write poetry because we are members of the human race. And the human race is filled with passion. So, medicine, law, business, engineering... these are noble pursuits and necessary to sustain life. But poetry, beauty, romance, love... these are what we stay alive for."

— Walt Whitman, Leaves of Grass

"You are a gold mine, hidden in earth, to purify you, we must set you on fire."

— Rumi

Trust the Process

This book is a journey from the deepest despair to the discovery of self-worth and our place in the universe. In life's darkest moments, when hope fades and willpower weakens, we often feel lost, burdened by the weight of existence. Faith slips away, and loneliness envelops us, making self-worth seem distant and unattainable. But it's in these moments of profound struggle that the seeds of transformation are planted.

No matter how far we stray from our roots, they inevitably call us back. Just as Saturn returns to its place in the universe, we too return to our true selves. Depression, like a volatile ether, can either be bottled up or released. In the quest for self-discovery, we learn that peace often comes not through victory, but through surrender—surrender to our own truth and inner self.

In the end, love and light guide us home. Piece by piece, we become whole again. Hope is reborn, and with it, the joy of discovering our true selves. This is a story of transformation, resilience, and the unwavering belief that, no matter how dark the night, the dawn always comes.

Chapters

The Great Malefic
The Cosmic Warrior
Saturn Return
The Karmic Cosmos
The Cosmic Homecoming

The Great Malefic

A shroud of darkness settles on my mind,
forms a cloud heavy with mighty rain.
Thundering beats echo in my heart,
pounding at my brain.
I see every thought turn into flesh,
skinning me alive,
burning with every breath.
How is it that I became so obsessed with the darkness?
Wasn't I all about the light?
Is it grief,
or was I born this way?
One of the many questions that keeps me awake.

The art of grieving

Sadness
crawled all over me like spiders
and I scratched myself raw.
Drenched in the flood of tears –
Grief again, pooled beneath my feet.
Even the rain tastes like tears.
My hands and cheeks are ordeal to
always and forever bed my fears.
Soaked and heavy
Limp and listless
Like me –
Of whom I've become
A person without a spine
In the end
I believe.
The sadness won
The web it wove –
is something I can never wrench myself free from.
It wasn't in my head.
At least,
It wasn't in my head.
It was real –
Yet surreal.

Let's talk about sadness.

The night fell,
And I fell apart.

With the sound of your voice
echoing in my heart

Hopeless romantic

We are fooled with the idea of tomorrow.
Tomorrow and tomorrow and tomorrow and tomorrow.
It's like a sigh.
It's impending abandonment.
It's waiting and it's inevitability.

Tomorrow

How do I get through the day?

I drag my wretched, wretched heart
tied to my feet.
A coffin rests on my shoulders,
with my soul sealed inside.

Take notes.

I am a magnet for chaos and suffering.
I invite terrible things to happen to me,
only to welcome pain as I would an old friend.

Sucker for chaos.

The sky resembles my heart so much,
As if it's made of similar elements.
The grey of the clouds mirrors my heart,
Filled with rain and lots of rage.
Soon, it is going to burst.
When it does,
it won't be just a quiet morning rain.
To soothe a suffering soul.
There will be dreadful lightning
and a thunder so loud it will shatter hearts to
bits and pieces. But all I wonder is, would there
be a rainbow after this hail?
Or just an unceasing thunder that abolishes
what remains?

Stop reading this book.

First came the pain
knocking at the door.
Then the realisation
barged in!
In the dense crowd
sat acceptance – in a corner.
Pushed back!
Forgotten.

Unwelcomed guests.

I heard a trembling voice from within,
a mere whisper,
it inquired,
"I delved into your soul. Shall I liken thee to a
frigid snowy night?"

The things I may be made of.

Mirror, mirror on the wall,
Who is the fairest of all?
Who is the prettiest of all?
You're not the one I think you should know,
Never ask this question again if you don't want to feel small.
The little I've travelled and the faces I've seen,
I can tell you; you are not pretty at all.

Mirror, mirror what is fair?
Why do I even care?
Mirror, mirror on the wall,
Who is the most pathetic of all?
You; delusional, imagining of living in a fantasy.
Maybe this is the reason you care.
Pathetic; I tell you; Pathetic of all; is the one
standing in front of me and thinks that a mirror
gives a damn at all.

Mirror, mirror, if I fall,
Would someone help me to stand tall?
No one from nowhere would come for you.
If you fall, you'll be gone,
Once and for all.

Mirror, mirror what I mean,
Is that I wish you could see.
I am much more than you believe.
If you believe,
You should be relieved.
And now it's time for you to know, I reflect, not reveal.

Mirror, mirror show my soul.
Because you're my friend so honest
Have the guts to gall.
I do not know about your soul,
I just know what you have told,

What your reflection possess is what's right.
That you have strength to fly,
 ignite the light and slay the demon
that lives inside.

Mirror, mirror I think you're the best of all.
You're ordinary, placed on an ordinary stonewall.
You have showed me a way to be a meteor.
Now please be there to pick me up when I fall.
Misery, fear whatever you see,
Lies inside you the thoughts that drown you not what you
see in me.
You shouldn't have let a mirror control your mirth,
As I can never dictate your true worth.

Mirror, Mirror

This eclipsed heart,
weary of its rhythms,
wearier of its wounds.

It asserts that endurance is a path,
a means to live,
and a way to survive.
But how much can I endure?
And for how long?
Until I draw breath?
Or until I cease to breathe?

Total Eclipse of the Heart!

I thought,
I am pure.
Never have I ever
thought how a little space
and an apostrophe can make a difference.
But the words carved under my skin
have a mind of their own.
My own skin screams my reality,
Calling the word that burns on me,

I'M PURE (without an apostrophe, without a space).

Scars have a mind of their own.
Gillian Flynn.

I'm in the cocoon of sadness, silence,
and darkness.
Grieving the loss of myself in a process called life.
Surrounded by immense happiness, yet imploding sorrow
caves in on me.
Someone's calling out my name, reaching for my hand.
Not just someone, but him,
Burning himself in the process.
I hear him say my name.
Almost sounding sweet, happy.

yet, there's a thin line between reality and fantasy.
How do I discern if it's happening in my mind or in
this existence?
It is excruciating to admit living in a fantasy while he
resides in reality.
Can't we just meet in the middle?

The great malefic indeed.

Let my silence embrace you,
For I have no heart to speak tonight.

I'm slowly disappearing into the cold, dark night,
As if a heavenly death is embracing me.
Silence has many words.
Only heard by those who are willing enough to listen.
Silence blooms like a flower
on the grave of those who suffered in the world of evil.

There's only agonising noise,
Silence,
With its words,
Speaks to me.
As it does, it asks me to stay silent,
Silent about the beautiful suffering,
About the joy of pain,
About the constant penetration of thorns in my heart.

If others were to hear,
They would wish for the same things,
Because you only miss the sun
When it's cold and dark.

Beautiful silence

A bed of roses peeked from my mouth
when I spoke to you last summer

Winter came,
and everything went cold,
so did I.
Now all that remains are thorns.

Raw and harmful
for you.

Yet beautiful
for me.

I'll chew your heart and spit it out.

I crave death, and it craves me.
It wonders what it would be like,
to finally embrace me.
I see it watching over my shoulders,
peeking from my door, making my room colder.
Sometimes, it drags me to the blade,
to watch me bleed and take me away.
Selfish.
So selfish.

Death hovers over me
when I take my goodnight pill.
"Have some more," it purrs,
Sitting beside me as I write.
Begging me to make this poem look good,
to make it rhyme,
because it may be my last.
Little did I know!
There is someone who wants me.
All of me, craves me,
and maybe, just maybe, needs me.
Little did I know!
It is death and decay.

Death, my best friend.

Things you say
are written on me.
Scarred on me, by me,
with the abused permanent ink.
The colour is blood,
so dark and deep.
When I sleep,
my words separate themselves from me
to go find their chroniclers,
abusing them and telling them
that your apology,
your begging,
your crying,
is not the cure.

Is your heart full of thorns?

I take things seriously.

I wonder what it's like
to sleep peacefully.
To just sink
into a deep slumber,
with even breaths.

Without sweet dreams,
nightmares,
cold sweat,
and a dry throat.
To just lie down on my bed,
to be grateful just for having this bed.
To put a bright smile on my face,
and sleep.

Just the way I grew up
watching Disney princesses sleeping on TV.
All I want is to see,
how it feels
to sleep peacefully.

Because when I lie on my bed,
there is a process that I go through,
I struggle
and scream at the voices to go away.

I try to escape the faces staring down at me.
I tame my chaos.
Calm my thunder.
Shut my eyes tight,
and beg for the voices to go away.

I cry as I write,
It is that hard.
I whine as I write,

It is that painful.
I fight with my mind,
as I write,
because I can't find the words
to describe the feeling.
I drown in my regrets as I try to sleep.
And I think that I think too much
and how my friends say I think too much
and tell me that I shouldn't.

How do I tell them?
It is the only survival instinct that I have left.

I see things floating in front of my eyes,
My shadow walking in front of me,
I imagine stars on my ceiling
that help my soul twinkle a bit,
And I hear them whispering
promises of tranquillity.

I find myself under a sky full of stars,
I escape again.
I see myself floating
into the world that I created in my mind.

I am by the shore now.
How peaceful it is to be
in his arms,
Under His protection,
in a cold breeze,
just me and my thoughts.

I close my eyes,
and I sleep.
In case you're wondering (or not).

I take things seriously.

I tiptoe around the trip wires
That the angry men in my house have set
I don't know which step would be the wrong step
Which breath would be the wrong breath
I avoided angry men as best as I could
Only to become an angry man myself
There is always one angry man in the house
I am the angry man of the house
My mother warned me if I didn't become the perfect epitome of a
woman
I will end up with an angry man
Mother, I am an angry man now
My mother also wished if I could just be much more feminine and try
to be beautiful and fair and polite and don't smile with my teeth and
never cut my hair
I will be fortunate to end up with a decent albeit infidel rich man
Mother, I am a rich man
And Mother, I am everything you asked me not to be
And feared that I would become.

Mother knows best

I reek of sadness.
Sometimes, I feel like I seek sadness even in the happiest places.
My mind always looks for an escape, a fire exit,
just the way I search for my favourite person in a crowd,
or try to catch the lyrics of my favourite song in a restaurant.

I snooze on the bitter reality.

When the soul is rotting from within,
There is no saving it.
No shell, no outer covering.
No disguise can hide it.
The stench of this blight
Emerges from the pores of my skin.
My mind smells like a cadaver.
No matter what I do,
The smell doesn't go away.
My body reeks of decay.

Rosewater baths have lost their effect.
My perfume strives to avoid my skin,
To not sense my essence.
My soul detests my existence.
Don't try to understand!
What's destroying my soul!

The place where once butterflies were born,
And lavender grew,
Once harboured hope.
It now smells like despair.
Even the air repels me,
When it touches me.
It shivers and cringes,
And the flowers.
Oh, the flowers.
They feel the pain of the air.
That it endures
When it touches
Someone like me.

I am no less than a cadaver.
The stench is becoming intolerable. Bury me.
My skin, my eyes, my heart and my mind want to leave me.
They want a life of their own
with someone who isn't me.

How do I tell them? I want the same thing.

I want to be someone who isn't me.

Happiness,
is such a happy word.
Certainly not made for a person like me.

The word dreads me.

I think I'm a coward
who prefers death over life.
I look for an escape
from the mess that I've made,
this mess that I call life.
I fail to grasp its beauty.
Ungrateful!
I have everything I could ever wish for but peace.
Ungrateful!
I desire invisibility
but
I crave attention.
Seems like
I'd rather choose to cease to exist
than accept who I am.

Ungrateful.

What if you wake up tomorrow and forget who you are?
What if the room is on fire and you keep thinking about getting your
shoes on?
What if the house is drowning and you just stand there frowning?
What if the storm is coming and you make a cup of tea to welcome it?
What if the person you love unloves you and you just watch it go
down?
What if the things you hate start to love you?
What if the things you left behind come crawling back to you?
What if the words you say to others find a way to come back to gnaw
at you?
What if you tremble and fear the unknown and you lose all hope?
What if the light that blinds you is the light of hell fire?
What if the height that scares you is the gate of heaven?
What if the stars that burn above are not stars at all?
What if the thoughts become fresh and haunt you forever?
What if your beloved dead ones you once loved comes back to life?
What if everyone is dead and it's just a ghost town?
What if the monsters that chained you beg you for help?
What if the demon dies on your doorstep?
What if the moon burns from the sunlight?
What if the stars shine so bright it looks like daylight?
What if the ocean in Pluto is the same as the ocean in Northside of
my country?
What if it was heaven and we made it hell?
What if the diamonds are salt pieces found by the dead?
What if sand is gold and gold is sand?
What if paper is money and money is all the paper we can have?
What if you become you and hate who you are?
Or worse, what if you become you and love who you are?
What if your friends make other friends and they make other friends,
and everyone lose friends?
What if this is just a moment, not life?
What if we are just a memory in someone's mind?
What if our thoughts are not ours?
What if the words are stolen and borrowed that we write for hours?

What if? What if? What if?

What if I'm not the hero in my own story?What if I don't get my
throne's glory?
What if the crown that I wear is made of bones and ashes?
What if the graveyard that I walk on grabs me and put latches?
What if the ghost under the bed now lives inside my head?
What if the wrong decisions I made led me to that
What if you kiss your mother's feet and go to heaven?
What if you bruise your father's pride and get eternal damnation?
What if the sweet whispers are of the spirits?
What if the wars they won were pyrrhic?
What if we take the right for wrong and wrong for right?
What if the sky is all colors and we are colorblind?
What if beneath the earth I get left behind while you enjoy the prom-
ised fruits of afterlife
What if the night engulfs the darkness inside
 What if the sun is a starry night
 What if in this endless fight, you forget what is right
 What if I tried to break your heart and broke mine instead?
What if the glass that shattered during the fight makes the comfiest
bed?
What if the tea splattered across the wall would be harder to clean
than the blood pooled on the floor?
What if I could trade the love of my life just to lie in mother's lap
once more?
What if the animal in me lashes out with wounded pride?
What if I could haunt your dreams for a lifetime?
What if I touched your scar and became you for a moment or so?
What if I clawed my way to heaven to only find the doors locked?
What if the devil snatches the key to the only door that brings you
peace?
What if my heirloom gets stolen and sold piece by piece?
 What if you turn yourself inside out
 What if you blink and time stops
 What if you become free and there's nothing left to ask for
 What if moon is burnt from the sunlight
 What if this brunt is taken by the twilight

  For a minute, let us think about a Saturday Night?
When the 'what if's' came to life, a blight of thoughts in a poem's
disguise.

What if? What if? What if?

I could let the sunlight fill the room.
I could let the sunlight fill my heart as it does the moon.
But I don't, and I won't.
Sadness has turned me into the deepest shade of blue,
the withered body turning crimson, so red it bleeds.
Tired hues all around me,
Smoke in the air turning black.
The blues of the sky merging with the yellow,
Ever-dissolving sight.
The sky palette – colour me.
It's hard staying bland tonight.
My heart might take flight.
Mind – already turned to blight.
Forgiveness lies plain in sight.
Essential to survive.
My stomach feels pointed to a knife.
Staying alive is the hardest tonight.

Sleep,
Sleep, my heart.
Don't steep so far.
Please. Please don't fall apart.
Even though it would be such an explicit art.
Nothing to be afraid of.
If you cannot suffer this much?
Then what the hell are you made for?
The faint of heart
won't survive this far.
It's the survival of the fittest,
and the game of the wittiest.
If you play, you play hard.
If you die, you die hard.
It's finally time to play your card.

The wisps of sadness on the lips of happiness.

Collecting scraps and scraps of life,
Clawing for it.
In this sore haze of defeat,
Ivy and wisteria wrap all over me.
How did I become a lighter shade of myself??
Fading into the daylight,
Day after day.

Collecting scraps

things will get better. things will get better. things will get better.
things will get better. things will get better. things will get better.
things will get better. things will get better. things will get better.
things will get better. things will get better. things will get better.
things will get better. things will get better. things will get better.
things will get better. things will get better. things will get better.
things will get better. things will get better. things will get better.
things will get better. things will get better. things will get better.
things will get better. things will get better. things will get better.
things will get better. things will get better. things will get better.
things will get better. things will get better. things will get better.
things will get better. things will get better. things will get better.
things will get better. things will get better. things will get better.
things will get better. things will get better. things will get better.
things will get better. things will get better. things will get better.
things will get better. things will get better. things will get better.
things will get better. things will get better. things will get better.
things will get better. things will get better. things will get better.
things will get better. things will get better. things will get better.
things will get better. things will get better. things will get better.
things will get better. things will get better. things will get better.
things will get better. things will get better. things will get better.
things will get better. things will get better. things will get better.
things will get better. things will get better. things will get better.
things will get better. things will get better. things will get better.
things will get better. things will get better. things will get better.
things will get better. things will get better. things will get better.
things will get better. things will get better. things will get better.
things will get better. things will get better. things will get better.
things will get better. things will get better. things will get better.
things will get better. things will get better. things will get better.
things will get better. things will get better. things will get better.
things will get better. things will get better. things will get better.
things will get better. things will get better. things will get better.

Mantra for the day

The Cosmic Warrior

Why be a moon?
When you can be the Saturn?
A universe – within a universe.
A world of unknown mysteries.
A world so far away,
where there is no warmth.
Far from being blemished by the sun.

The cosmic warrior.

Keep your voices low
as I suffer in silence.
Believe me when I say
I need to lay low tonight.
Tonight is a hard night.
I just need it to pass.
I may die a little
but I will not die.
I will only turn to dust.
I may stay cold and keep shivering
on a cold marble floor
that sinks me in
every single time I take a breath.
With the water dripping from the tap.
Torture, I must say.
I need to be alone.
I need to stay high as I lay low tonight.

Tonight,
the world, stars, galaxy, and the moon witnessed as I broke into
pieces.
Believe me when I tell you,
there is no fixing it.
Not anymore.
Embarrassing.
Painful.
Hard.
That's what it is.

Reality check: I fantasise about fantasising.

Reality check: It must stop.

When I grasp the slippery reality
and come back to the real world,
I am broken.

No, broken does not even describe it,
let me walk you through it.
Until you see what I see.
Until you feel what I feel.

Believe me when I say,
you cannot live in my shoes even for an hour.
I may not be able to live in yours.

First: the sky isn't that blue as I imagined it to be
and as I expected it to be.

Second: The sun tries to burn me.

It is okay; only a few are worth getting burned.

Third: There is no one around.

Comfort, people, and peace that existed in my mind,
Gone.

Reality check: I must stop living inside my mind

I step into reality.
And I see my mother crying.
I see my father crying.
I see my brother and sister crying.
Begging for the peace and happiness that does not exist.

How do I tell them what I have always known?

Which brings me to:

Fourth: the only place where the happiness that I want exists is in my
rotting delusional fantasising mind.

Reality check: The voices that I hear that tell me what to do and nar-
rate my whole life for me are only inside my head.

As I go wandering in my mind,
I visit the forbidden places.
I sit down there.
And I wonder what it feels like to be in the reality.

Which brings me to

Fifth: Reality feels like suffering.

Believe me when I tell you,
life is not just a journey.
It's a journey of suffering.
A valley of excruciating pain.
A dungeon where lies only darkness.
Which brings me to

Sixth: the kind of love I crave, and the love that I want to give,
only exists in
you know where.

The cosmic warrior.

Soak your feet in the blood,
the blood that you bled into the drain,
the blood of your suffering and pain.

This blood is black with no compassion.
No purity.
It has a void.
A void that demands
this fragile heart of yours.

Tell your heart!
Oh you impure piece of irrational art,
"Fill that void of mine,
so it doesn't tear me apart."

Pain and its synonyms.

It's never being in the now
that weighs me down the most.
It's either dreading the future
or digging the corpses of the past.
It's the unpredictability of this life.
Never letting the dead – die.
Never letting the past slip from my hands like sand.
But holding onto it like mud.
Moulding it into something it's not.
The past seems so pure sometimes
in the back of my mind –
Like snow falling from the seventh sky.
When reality sets in –
The snow turns into shards of ice.
And I'm stabbed everywhere I turn.
Is today nothing? Whitman asks.
Today has never been anything.
It's either yesterday or tomorrow.
It's never today for me.
I never lived in today.
Wouldn't it change everything?
Why would I change anything?
To know that today – now, I'm here.
It would be an insufferable pain – to acknowledge.
To be here and yet be nothing
The living are palpable –
Today is palpable.
Today is a palpable sense of loss.

Now.

Hello, old cold marble floor!
We are in deep touch again.

When I lifted myself up,
And mended and stitched myself
to make it through the day.
I didn't take it slow, no
I rose again,
Should've gone step by step.
But ran steep by steep instead.
To a place far away
where echoed only my name.
I prostate to thank God
and saluted the sun.
The reason for which I rose up.
I bent down to pick a shiny little pebble
and collected many to make a heap.
I made a mountain of my own.
Forgot, there is such a thing as sleep.
As my mountain awaited
I climbed up,
up to the clouds
to reach the sky
Oblivious to fail
Oblivious to fall
Oblivious to hurt
I slipped from the first pebble
that shined up to me
that helped me create a mountain
I fell down, down to the ground
and landed on the old cold marble floor
And I wait
to witness the process of my slow death.

I am dying, slowly, so slowly.

And I hope, pray, wish
that my dreams are not shattered into nothing
maybe they're just crumpled like pieces of paper
they are not doomed
I can fix them
there will be blurred lines
but at least I will still have dreams.

Farsighted and farfetched.

Ammi telling me to keep my feet clean – or it would leave marks!
How right she was.
To be aware of where you step
or you'll get hurt.
To protect your feet
even when walking on the soft grass
Be aware of thorns.
Don't stomp, float.
She said – don't ever walk barefoot.
Wear the flower.
Wear a crown instead of a frown.
Whenever I showed her my new clothes, she said how long they'd
last?
Wish I could tell her how right she was.
I remember Ammi singing a song in a language I didn't understand.
Telling a tale of how her finger got broken once when caught up be-
tween a fight of two bulls.
She told me never to intervene in a fight between animals or worse –
humans.
Ammi always smelled of motia.
She decorated her ears with it,
the only jewellery she ever wore.
She preferred flowers over ornate jewels.
Abbu told me to recite the Quran for the peace of heart.
In the darkest hour of the night.
Ask for the message.
And you'll receive one.
Read – what it says, what it means.
Call upon Him, He'll answer you.

Forgotten and untested Lessons of Childhood.

Breaking and entering,
Opening and enlightening,
Made of earth so raw,
Scorching lava underneath,
Rainwater storm and lightning,
Thunderclaps, torrents,
Forever frightening.
The trees that bear the paper,
Has essence of each.
It now bleeds with me,
Leaves glisten with pride.
The dew drops absorb the sunlight.
The eyes are just shallow,
From watering the roots all night.
Tree has the essence,
The bark knows what's to come.
The paper becomes absorbent enough.
Feel everything.
Dissolve into nothingness.
A place called life.
A palace called feelings.
A memory – oblivious.
A regret – inevitable.
The beginning is an ending.
The ending – a birth.
How often death overcomes mind?
How life begins when death's in sight?
Whatever it is I'm made of,
Will forever be mine.
Even if it's a pinch of salt,
A tablespoon of mercury,
Or a mountain of kimberlite.
My love, my love,
I'll be soft as a marshmallow,
A melancholic tender love,
Dissolved, blushed and melted when tasted.

If you don't treat me well,
You'll have no throat to swallow.
You'll find me as bitter as truth.
Roll me in a blanket,
When I talk about him,
Or losing him.
Or finding Him.
Or death.
I'm not only talking about it,
I'm wondering,
And wandering,
And it's a dangerous combination.

Lose the creation, find the Creator!

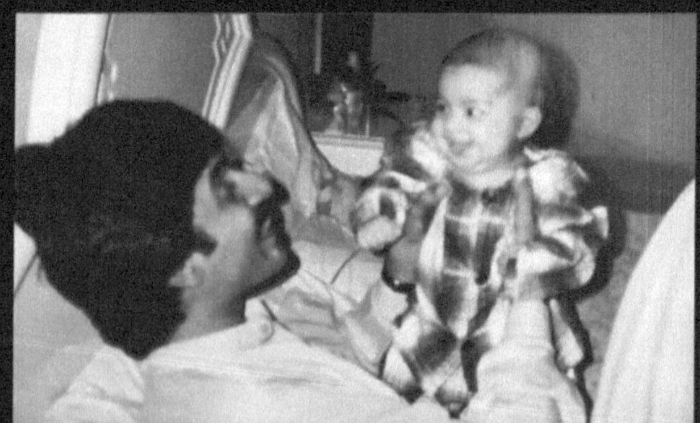

The sound of my mother's bangles,
Hums the sweet forgotten song of childhood.
When I try to remember — it takes me to a galaxy far far away.
Where I taste milk and honey.
I hear a sweet melancholic lullaby.
It voices and choirs and echoes her sufferings.
Little did my mother know,
That in the darkest of nights, the sound of her bangles
Chased my demons away.
They knew.
Someone exists who loves me unconditionally
and that kind of love, unwittingly creates a boundary of protection.
Whatever wicked comes my way will suffer an unimaginable death.

Such an unconquerable soul.

And I will forever wish to see my father again
only without the worry lines etched
— stretched across his face.
What I remember best from the last time I saw him,
is the pride and happiness I brought forth with my presence
in his life.
I think his kiss on my forehead,
would always come to me as a mixture of
shock, surprise and utter delight.
We only get a single set of parents,
And for the life of me,
I will wish for them in this or any other lifetime.

"You look like your father"

When I was shattered,
People who I thought cared about me started to pick up the pieces
which, they thought were the best of me.
When I thought, they were going to put back the pieces to their accus-
tomed places,
how wrong was I?

Little did I know!
They kept it for themselves.
For they were,
The best
Pieces of me

I'm a left over.

Sadness comes with the same spirit as joy.
And I can do nothing but enjoy.
I love the spirit in both forms.
It makes my heart race.
One makes me feel weak in the knees.
The other gives me butterflies.
When I am complete with this spirit,
I try to remember how being empty feels like.

Suffering is beautiful in its own way.

My translated screams.
Scriptures of my encrypted dreams.
My heart, my soul, my wounded mind,
My lips, my eyes, my clouded cries.
The silent screams and loud whispers.
The drenched shirt and soaked eyes.
The tear-stained pillows under starry nights.
With nothing left in me to fight.
Afraid to see myself.
Afraid of what's inside.
Will it bite?
It's fight or flight.
Fight or flight.
Fight or flight.
Fight or flight.
Think. Think. Think. I thought.
The lighter I felt, the darker I got.
Weight that I lifted off
Came stomping at my chest.
It feels like that story.
Once told by my mother.
A nightmare so calm.
It pulls me to a deep slumber.
A dream so heavy,
It jerks me awake.
The pain from the stakes
Oh, for goodness' sake!
It's not that bad.
As I make myself believe.
Breathe. Breathe. Breathe. I failed.
I shouldn't feed my poetry such lies.
I should never speak.
The whimpers of
my wounded animalistic existence,
Screams to destiny.
What lies in eternity?
What is that?

What will set me free?
Should I have done this?
When I did that?
Is this what anxiety feels like?
Or is there another word for it?
Or is it just a cliché?
The butterflies in my stomach,
Have turned to ashes.
I feel plants growing underneath.
With flowers I've never seen
With a touch of heaven
And a little bit of sin
Never have I ever let myself think.
Even though I knew that life would end in just a blink.
Do I know you as much as you know me?
Or am I too self-consumed to even let you breathe?
Am I taking too much of your breath away?
That it makes it difficult to see me
Or is it just a methodological play?

This game.

It's all just sorrow tainted by joy.
Why me? Why me? Why me?
The question remains.
The heart gives out.
But sorrow decides to stay.
I could, I would, and I will be.
Anything and everything that is thrown at me.
Any trouble that comes and embraces me.
I give in, I give up and I let it be.
It's skin over skin over skin over skin.
Kith and kin of sorrow and everything within.
Light and dark and the wistful melancholia.
Twirls around together in an intimate dance.
Undress and let it all fall down.
Skin after skin after skin after skin.
Undress and see what remains.
When the sorrow is nothing but rags of clothing.
What is it that you are without your sorrow? Tell me.
Is it sin? Is it joy? Is it tragedy? or is it emptiness?
Something as emptiness taking so much space,
seems ironic how heart allots rooms to its tenants.

Sorrow Sorrow Sorrow

I try to escape therapy
because I am a hoarder of grief and its friends
because I am afraid of letting things go
I'm afraid of a steady heartbeat
a normal sleep,
a dreamless slumber,
a night free from nightmares,
a lifeless life
no illusions,
no delusions,
a stable, normal breathing,
an ordinary thinking pattern
I'm afraid of being ordinary
I'm nothing but I'm afraid of going into nothingness
and I'm afraid of admitting that I'm afraid.

Do I contradict myself? Very well then, I contradict myself.

And maybe, just one day,
the sun decides to stop giving light to the moon.

And maybe, just one day,
the sun decides not to shine and stops giving light at all.
Feeling tired of only giving.

And maybe, just one day,
the moon decides to shine on its own.
And when it does,
it makes the sun, shine again.

And on that day,
the stars will witness it all.
It will remind them of you and me.
That how I lost my shine and took yours away too.
And how you shined all by yourself.
And gave all your light to me.

Sunbathing in the moonlight.

I stood mortified.
You left, satisfied.
I see my life slipping right before my eyes.
I have nothing to hold on to.
Maybe I saw right through you.
Maybe I was holding on to a mirage of you.
And it's clear now.
Like the blue sky after it rains.
And it's brighter now.
Like the sun I see stretching from my windowpane.
And it's lighter now.
Now, that the pain parachuted from my heart.
I can seek now.
Whatever I was willing to find.

I feel happy after writing sad poetries.

I wish I could rip my heart out
and dip and soak it in the Noor
that falls upon me at the time of dawn.

A *way to purify.*

It feels like I'm threaded to hell.
Maybe that's why I burn so much.
Because surely Noor wouldn't feel like that.
It wouldn't make me grind my teeth so much
my face is always hot
with anxiety
with loss of purpose.

Hellfire or Noor?

I can roam into my mind.
But not the streets of my city at night.
Or in bright daylight.
There are monsters that chase our skins.
With their lusts and all their kith and kin.
There are beasts that can scent the blood.
And seek us through the wind.
And when they find us.
They find us and they aim to kill.
Hit the nerves where it hurts.
Touch and torture and sin.
Until they win.

Wolves in lamb's clothing.

I walk in the forest full of lions.
I swim the sea full of sharks.
It's a bloodbath everywhere.
It's the city I live in.
I'm seen as a bait,
but the city has forged me into a trap.
It's not the fire that you ignite.
It's the fire that is inside.
It's not the way that you thrive.
It's the way you survive.

I want to untangle my brain and wipe all the stains.

You leave a kind of lethargy –
When you leave.
It's the same kind when I sleep.
Into a dreamless dream
After the endless chase
Like a hamster in a wheel.
When do I stop?
When do I say 'enough'?
This can never be repeated.
A slumber of darkness erupts.
Sucking me in
Although I know I shouldn't
But I lean in
It's been so long since I wrote something worth reading.
Do I miss the blood? The pain? The endless joy? Or the endless weep-
ing?
A cynical crime,
And a road that never ends.
Would I bleed?
Or would I just end?

Chase.

The poet in me died
When you left the door ajar
In a bleak winter night
The blood rushed
In the veins
The cause of highs,
That caused the pain.
It froze.
By the cold embrace
and I kept weeping
with never ending sadness
But wait -
But wait -

The chills that kill.

What am I supposed to do with this sugar-coated sadness?
What am I supposed to do with my left-over self?
I devoured the love that you gave me.
I am exhausted with all the love I gave.
No more of that left, please come back tomorrow when I replenish.
Brace yourself for the sadness that is to come.
The lashing hail.
The imperious pain.
Sharpen your knives for the fight that is to come!
Clear your throat to have a debate with the regret that will barge
through your front door.
Will I peel myself to the bone to forget how he feels?
I smell like him, and he smells like me.
And you ask, who is to blame?
The air or the affair?
The bed stays warm - he reeks of beautiful comfort.
I wear a fragrance of regret.
Dressed as what jealously looks like
The middle part of the bed that parts us
It cleaved a black hole.
It will sink the one who makes the first move to forgive.
It will make a home underneath the skin of the one who won't.
It will shape itself into guilt and regret.
The creepiest best of friends
I belong to the darkest pits.
Where the spiders crawl and the sinners brawl
You belong to the brightest of meadows under the greenwood
shadow with songs of Heavens and Earth.
You float down from the sky.
I rise from the ground.
You're the midnight summer sadness.
I am the early riser downtown.
You say we belong.
But where and why?
I shadow the brightest of skies.
I seek the darkness in the light.
I dig a grave to rest in every night.

I cry with all the happiness lying by my side.
I sin to make it to the lion's den.
I sin to see myself repent.
I sin to see how this will end.
You brighten up the darkest pit.
You stay with me through all this darkness.
You ask me to stay still.
To love in excess, is to love to kill.
You swallow up the smoke.
So, I can breathe and stay alive.
I know you'd starve yourself.
So that I can survive.

You will stay with me even when I beg to repent.
You will stay with me even in the lion's den.
You will stay with me even when I sin to the brink of death.
You will stay with me till my last breath.
I hope you and I never get to see how it ends.

Sugar-coated midnight sadness.

In daylight I walk as a shadow of myself
Blending and bleeding and bending
However,
I moonlight as a poet
Forever the poet,
Never the poem
This very delighted
Lighthearted me
Ever the saint
having affair with the sins
In love with the Ideation of love
Mortality is a sin
Morality a joke
But when it comes to cowardice no one wins other than hope

Moonlighting.

the pain will end. the pain will end. the pain will end. the pain will end.
the pain will end. the pain will end. the pain will end. the pain will end.
the pain will end. the pain will end. the pain will end. the pain will end.
the pain will end. the pain will end. the pain will end. the pain will end.
the pain will end. the pain will end. the pain will end. the pain will end.
the pain will end. the pain will end. the pain will end. the pain will end.
the pain will end. the pain will end. the pain will end. the pain will end.
the pain will end. the pain will end. the pain will end. the pain will end.
the pain will end. the pain will end. the pain will end. the pain will end.
the pain will end. the pain will end. the pain will end. the pain will end.
the pain will end. the pain will end. the pain will end. the pain will end.
the pain will end. the pain will end. the pain will end. the pain will end.
the pain will end. the pain will end. the pain will end. the pain will end.
the pain will end. the pain will end. the pain will end. the pain will end.
the pain will end. the pain will end. the pain will end. the pain will end.
the pain will end. the pain will end. the pain will end. the pain will end.
the pain will end. the pain will end. the pain will end. the pain will end.
the pain will end. the pain will end. the pain will end. the pain will end.
the pain will end. the pain will end. the pain will end. the pain will end.
the pain will end. the pain will end. the pain will end. the pain will end.
the pain will end. the pain will end. the pain will end. the pain will end.
the pain will end. the pain will end. the pain will end. the pain will end.
the pain will end. the pain will end. the pain will end. the pain will end.
the pain will end. the pain will end. the pain will end. the pain will end.
the pain will end. the pain will end. the pain will end. the pain will end.
the pain will end. the pain will end. the pain will end. the pain will end.
the pain will end. the pain will end. the pain will end. the pain will end.
the pain will end. the pain will end. the pain will end. the pain will end.
the pain will end. the pain will end. the pain will end. the pain will end.
the pain will end. the pain will end. the pain will end. the pain will end.
the pain will end. the pain will end. the pain will end. the pain will end.
the pain will end. the pain will end. the pain will end. the pain will end.

Saturn Return

Getting hold of old habits
of digging crescents into my palm.
I believe – it's better to be a lost planet
and appear as you please
than being a cold one with plenty of moons to deal with.
And like the moony planet, I live under the shell of rings of ice and
rocks.
It is said that nine of the Earths can make one Saturn
but hundreds of Saturns cannot make one me.
The great malefic.
Cold, distant,
a universe within a universe.
Just like Saturn, I'm lost again,
and just like Saturn, I will return.

Saturnine life, a lie.

Death comes at my bedside,
in the middle of the night
creeps through the darkness.

'What is it?' I asked.
'I came to greet an old friend,' said Death.
'Friends don't take what we cherish the most. Is it time?' I asked.
'You tell me? Is life good?' said Death.
'You look how I feel, so how good can it be?' I said.
'I tasted you, you're bitter.' said Death.
'I demanded you, you're stubborn', I replied.

Death whispers its secrets in my head.
And I can't help but feel as if all my life
I have been dead,
Yet living here with great regret.

Death and its friends.

In the darkness,
you held my face
and pointed it to the right direction.
You told me to follow the stars.
To not only lurk in the darkness,
But to look for the moonlight, starlight,
in the darkest of midnight.
You told me to learn a lesson from darkness
that how it existed before light.
How to feel happy in the reality.
You taught me that.
One thing you never taught me is,
how to live without you.

Love, an act of escapism!

Shattered but whole,
with a wilting ego I walk under the scorching sun,
Making it all about myself
Thinking –
I am the centre of the Earth and everything spins around me.
I feel the gaze of people piercing through my skin.
Crawling under my flesh and bones.
Carving words on my body of a language foreign to me.
My own self shouts at me
– abusing.
Look who's trying to fit in now!
I keep cotton candy in my mouth so I speak sweet
– I spill honey.
So you never get the taste of the words I say and how I say them.
Or I say nothing at all.
But the taste of my silence is bitter sweet.
When I stay silent, my silent eyes pierce through you.
And you become crystal clear to me.
And my body decides to leave me alone.
I'm just matter,
who matters.
Just a floating soul in space.
I am made of little bits of sand.
Mashed and blended
with acid rain.
That makes me whole
and when I rise up again
I'll devour you whole.
That is how I know,
How to be whole again,
after being completely shattered.

I am made of sugar, spice, and everything not nice.

Everything is up for grabs,
but it's intangible.
You collect the scraps,
expecting the impossible.
Crafting your sanity,
a testament of your pain.
What has been learnt in life?
Whatever that was gained.
The purpose – missing purpose,
what are you living for?
If you don't live for anything,
what will you die for?
It's a question of pride,
Explored to survive.
To live such a life,
where you can't deny.
The ecstasies of constant thrive.
Like Venus you burn – Like Icarus you run.
In this life where death is only a breath away.
Even if it's a second, don't waste it anyway.
Believe me you don't want to live in confinement.
You would resent your way of resigning.
Step out, explore.
Wander, implore.
Whatever it is, dive deeper!
Be a seeker – Live to see the days of life.
It's as easy as walking on a sharp-edged knife.

Before you go.

I swear I saw moonlight dancing,
just the way my heart danced
the night you said you love me.

What are you made of?

And every now and then
I ask you to take me to the sky
you say, 'We're on our way.'
'We'll find a way.'
It's just like patting a child on his head
Giving false hopes
'You'll be happy when you grow up'.

You and I.

And then there was this very strange December,
When I crawled out of the pits of sadness, despair, and endless melancholy.
Misery, it faded away.
My inner calamity turned to ashes.
Like a phoenix about to rise –
I rose into a new year.
Left only memories.
Scars.
Already healing.
Depression faded away like ether in the air.
I wish I could realise it before
How volatile this thing is.
Why shouldn't I write about it?
This is history.
It needs to be told.
This is the becoming.
An unfolding.
An opening.
Let the air find its way to my lungs!
Let the light find its way to my heart!
And the songs universe has to croon in my ears.
Let it be.
The abysses of anguish I had for eyes.
Are already filled with colossal starlight.
Flickering immense joy and gratification.
It's not more than a miracle.
That I found happiness in my heart.
The happiness that only existed in my mythical and delusional thoughts.
Glazed with strange caprices and whims.
This honey pouring happiness.
I hope it lasts.
Maybe not forever.
But at least for a while.
A treasured guest.
An imperative courtier in my perishable heart.

When the blood dries, a new day shines.

When Earth welcomes you yet again after your last sigh,
this is forgiveness.
Forgiveness of the crimes and mines you planted,
and made Earth witness.
Still, it welcomes you,
with your stench so bad,
with the weight of your guilt,
your pride,
your wilt.
Earth takes and takes,
and you do not yield pleasantries.
Even after all this time,
When Earth embraces you.
It makes you beautiful!
It makes you beautiful!
The colour green, the grass and vines.
With dew drops that shine.
It makes you look pretty.
Even though you made it feel ugly,
you bruised and battered the land.
Yet the same land,
it grows you.
It makes you bloom.
While your friends and foes walk over you.
It makes Earth pity that no one is witty.
But Earth is forgiveness.
It gives and it gives.
And yet you yield agonies.
The friend Earth once was becomes the foe.
With nothing left but woe.
But still you would return to it,
or where else you would go?

Care for the universe, because you are the universe.

The moon goes into hiding
with no beauty in sight.
The moon eclipses as it deems fit.
Sadly, I cannot depend on gazing the moon to cure my heart's afflic-
tion.
It will come back in due time because of its addiction.
Even when the moon comes back — I wish,
Your telescopic sight would turn in my direction instead.
Whenever you say the moon is looking magnificent.

I am a moon, and it's just a phase.

Be the moon when you want to
But,
Be the sun when you must.
And remember,
The sun has no shadow of its own.

The sun-moon stories.

Where does a thought go when you forget it,
It seeps within you till you regret it.
Where does a memory go when you coax it,
it dives deep into your bones till you hoax it?
You live a life of envy, with pride.
Fretting, that it's the only way to survive.
To merely live, till you inevitably die.
– is all that you can leave behind.

Memories.

Sometimes, I wonder if my heart is like a black hole.
So dense that there is no room for Noor.
I wonder if it will suck me in or just —

It's dark inside.

Morning
It has a certain breeze.
The breeze that has an eloquent voice
A voice that is trying to make me quiet.
As I turn quiet,
I can hear everything that the universe has to say to me.

Filled with sunshine, dandelion fluffs on my mind!

The moon watched and envied her, as she cried galaxies.

My eyes have become a galactic ocean.

I used to loathe the mirror
As it told me the truth
Never sugar-coated anything
Like the mirror in my house,
I should loathe you too
But I cannot bring myself to do so,
you, like the mirror, can be trusted to hold beauty
And truth
I asked the mirror
To show me what is true
When I finally built up the courage to look at it
All I could see was, you
As broken as me
As full of life as me
I could see the madness
I could see the sadness
The wild in you
The child in you
I remember asking God
For a friend
For life
With kindness in her eyes
And heart full of love and light
For I underestimated God,
When I asked for a friend
That is to say, he gave me so much more than I could ever ask for
Your name now ends up
In my gratitude list every night

If only!

A spark ignites as I wish to live,
like the break of dawn,
piercing through the darkness of my heart.
That spark, burns the darkness
like a ring of fire
ruthlessly conjuring my heart.
My soul, witnesses an intruder,
like a diamond-ring effect
at the end of a solar-eclipse.

Ring of fire

Light came looking for me after years,
told me – it forgot its way to my heart.
It confused my numbness for death.

My heart built mirrors around it to escape light.

Voices demand my silence.
They have a mind of their own.
I demand to desire.
A desire to call nothing my own.

What if I reached my best version?

Rose gold, lilac and pretty pretty pink.
Sweetness and cotton candy and happiness akin.
Apples and all the curses they bring.
Eyes with death and darkness within.
Promises of peace and never endings.
The blues, the hues and the endless ruse.
The eyes that hope versus the eyes that deceive.
One wins the battles, but the other wins the war.
If loving you will be the death of me,
then death is what I will embrace happily.
If kissing you will put me in the grave,
then not kissing you would be a grave mistake.
Lips call to lips.
Like calls to like.
No one can make this up.
It's fate – it's destiny.
It is how it will be for all eternity.
For the archer there always will be a prey.
But it's the choice that matters the most,
that the archer has to make.
To love, to kill, to spare, to care.
What is darker than the secrets you keep?
It's the hope of love that you see in me.
and all the things I can never be for you.
But I have enough hope for the both of us.
You held me like a secret,
I held you like hope.
Impossible ever after,
Is not what I asked for.
Merriment or misery.
It's a decent love affair.
But all of it would never matter,
If you despise a happy end.

I hope you brought enough apples.

Here I go,
I pick up my pen,
My quill,
My ink,
And I dive into the happiest memories of
the person who defined happiness for me.
And the words elude me
but I have enough peace she gave me – preserved
to delude me,
I would trade the sun for her
Since, she's better than sunlight anyway
And with her gone,
There would be no sun.
No light, no life, no sunshine
And
No sunflowers
and life is nothing, nothing, without sunflowers

She's the lens I look through
Rose-tainted glass
And it seems so much better this way
She's the calm in the midst of lightning
She is the simplest,
Yet
The most complex person I've ever met
And I will bet my favourite book,
My most comfortable nook,
And my peace of mind
That
This is the simplest
Most complex poetry you'll ever find
For she is the most difficult poetry I have ever had to write
Because it's not that she is difficult to comprehend
It's that you don't have that mind to understand
It's not that she can't be the darkest night
It's that you will be blinded by her etching sunlight

She looks like my favourite poetry book incarnate
That I memorised,
And whenever she talks
It feels like coming home to a familiar, loving warmth
I thought peace evaded me
She thinks peace can never be given
Like hand-outs
But what she gives me
Is her time and little does she know
It's always
Wrapped in peace
Like the stars cuddled with the clouds
Silence and violence
It makes a good combination when it comes to us
She rages against the dying light
It's all contained in a beautiful mind
It's like a solved mystery that still cannot be contemplated
It will and shall go down in history
For she has read as many lives
As she has lived

She has proven to be that peace
That comes after the war
The poppy that grows
On a barren land after a yearlong battle
If you're the lost ship
she's the star that will guide you home
Her love is like freshly baked bread
And blueberries
You cannot get enough of
Loneliness is abused by the idea of the friendship she offers
Age old scars fade away
By her healing hands
Age-worn sadness scurried away
When she came along

Sunflower

If I only had more time,
What would I have done?
Found eternal peace –
Or a way to stay eternally numb.

If I only had more words,
What would I have written?
A eulogy to hope?
Or a famous quote?

If I only had more breath?
What would I have breathed in?
Breeze of dawn?
The smell of rain and Earth?
Or the scent of your skin?

If I only had more patience,
What would I have endured?
The constant heartache?
Or the endurance of self-afflicted pain?

If I only had more love,
What would I have loved?
The elements that make up the world
Or the elements that made you up?

If I only had more ink
What would I have articulated?
A song that was sung
when the earth was bred?
Or the song that I sang for you,
when we were lying in our bed?

If I only had a few more pages?
What would I have drawn?
The world as it ages?
Or you, in each of your stages?

If I only had more tears,
What would I cry for?
The fact that you love me.
Or the fact you'd only love me till your heart stopped?

If I only had more paint
What would I have painted?
A Starry Night? The Nightmare? The Persistence of Memory? The
Boulevard Montmartre at Night? Or a depiction of Shakespeare's
Midnight Summer Dream?
Or would I paint you, shining in my darkest of nights and hushing
my screams?

If I only had another friend
What would I say to make it last till the end?
Nothing, nothing will ever be said.
The words kill the joy of silence, beats the friendship till its dead.

If I only had more blood
Who would I shed it for?
The country that is soaked in red
Or for the people who are already dead?

If I only had more books
What would I have read?
The Forty Rules of Love? Rumi?
Or whatever Whitman's poetry suggests.

If I only had more strength
What would I use it for?
To fight for the God given women rights
Or to get up from the bed?

If I only had more sadness
What would I be sad about?
The realities of the world
Or how much more can I be sad about.

If I only had more trust
Who would I rely upon?
A romantic interest?
Or the mother whose ageing doesn't stop.

If I only had more hate
What would I hate to have written in my fate?
The hell's gate?
Or the grasp I lost from my slippery faith?

If I only had more time.
What would I spend it on?
Would I have made this poem rhyme?
Or would I have wasted it forevermore?

If I had more time, I wouldn't mind.

Today is a good day. Today is a good day. Today is a good day.
Today is a good day. Today is a good day. Today is a good day.
Today is a good day. Today is a good day. Today is a good day.
Today is a good day. Today is a good day. Today is a good day.
Today is a good day. Today is a good day. Today is a good day.
Today is a good day. Today is a good day. Today is a good day.
Today is a good day. Today is a good day. Today is a good day.
Today is a good day. Today is a good day. Today is a good day.
Today is a good day. Today is a good day. Today is a good day.
Today is a good day. Today is a good day. Today is a good day.
Today is a good day. Today is a good day. Today is a good day.
Today is a good day. Today is a good day. Today is a good day.
Today is a good day. Today is a good day. Today is a good day.
Today is a good day. Today is a good day. Today is a good day.
Today is a good day. Today is a good day. Today is a good day.
Today is a good day. Today is a good day. Today is a good day.
Today is a good day. Today is a good day. Today is a good day.
Today is a good day. Today is a good day. Today is a good day.
Today is a good day. Today is a good day. Today is a good day.
Today is a good day. Today is a good day. Today is a good day.
Today is a good day. Today is a good day. Today is a good day.
Today is a good day. Today is a good day. Today is a good day.
Today is a good day. Today is a good day. Today is a good day.
Today is a good day. Today is a good day. Today is a good day.
Today is a good day. Today is a good day. Today is a good day.
Today is a good day. Today is a good day. Today is a good day.
Today is a good day. Today is a good day. Today is a good day.
Today is a good day. Today is a good day. Today is a good day.
Today is a good day. Today is a good day. Today is a good day.
Today is a good day. Today is a good day. Today is a good day.
Today is a good day. Today is a good day. Today is a good day.
Today is a good day. Today is a good day. Today is a good day.
Today is a good day. Today is a good day. Today is a good day.

Mantra for the Dawn

The Karmic Cosmos

My death — It can free me
in unimaginable ways that are hard to fathom
my soul will fly, screeching out of my body like a bird freed from its
cage,
free from the human made boundaries, only sky is the limit
this becoming — it will unleash my desires of what I truly call life
I will dissolve in the grains of sand
dive into the deepest ocean, never to return, never to breathe
I'll stand between the sun and the moon
and live among Pleiades
be weightless, colourless
and burn with the north star.

My heart — won't know any limits.

When I dwell between these two worlds,
I don't understand what I am anymore.

We are all suffering in our own exquisite ways.

Help!
I'm broken again.
I sheltered myself for a long time.
Under love, pleasure and vanity.
Solitude,
I made it my solace.
My being was complete.
But I am broken again

Help!
I am broken again.
I cannot put into words the pain I feel.
When I listen to Chasing Cars or Habits
When I think about Finch
When I think about the friends who left me because of my ego and
pride.

My harsh words and rudeness
I cannot put my pain into words.
But I can make you picture it.
It's like someone is peeling my flesh layer by layer and seasoning it
with salt and pepper to burn it even more, to make me feel the pain.
Someone is peeling my whole skin till nothing is left, only bones
which I am often mocked to be.

Either turn this page or burn this page.

Is this a good life?
Or a great lie?
Or a beginning of a happy ending?
Should I stay or should I go?
Going is inevitable,
So, I must stay.

Welcome to the world, we are all here to die.

Never have I ever played a game that I liked,
Never have I ever liked the games that I had to play,
Never have I ever run in a parade,
Never have I ever barged through the front gates.
Never have I ever escaped reality.
Never have I ever faced reality.
Never have I ever had a meeting with a ghost.
Never have I ever offered it tea.
Never have I ever got to say goodbye.
Never have I ever lived into the night.
Never have I ever wished to survive.
Never have I ever not wished to die.
Never have I ever been someone's dream.
Never have I ever lived my own dream.
Never have I ever enjoyed a nightmare.
Never have I ever liked your ugly stare.
Never have I ever cherished my fate.
Never have I ever appreciated my face.
Never have I ever been to a party

Never have I ever been drunk head to toe
Never have I ever danced to a slow song.
Never have I ever have thought about that for long.
Never have I ever unloved a person.
Never have I ever un-smelled a smell.
Never have I ever drunk the moonlight.
Never have I ever kissed a starlight.
Never have I ever stepped on the moon.
Never have I ever wanted to die so soon.
Never have I ever wanted to last forever.
Never have I ever asked for this pain that I everyday endeavour,
Never have I ever begged for forgiveness.
Never have I ever meant to forgive.
Never have I ever lost a true friend.
Never have I ever craved more than one true friend.
Never have I ever cared truly.
Never have I ever owned a sweater that is woolly.
Never have I ever, played never have I ever.
Because I never would ever play a game that I have already lost.

Never have I ever.

To my brother,
I wish I could taste my words before spitting them out
like flaming daggers
that pierced your heart.
And something there shattered.
Something related to me.
Maybe love, or respect.
Or trust
I only wish to gain it back
someday.

Swallowing my tongue.

To my sister,
she is my saviour
I wish I could be hers
I know what it's like to have a sister
who protects me with whatever she has
burning to make me see the light.

Mercury blinded by the etching sunlight.

Never stop sowing seeds of kindness into your skin.
Into your mind,
Into your heart,
Into your art.
Never stop!
Never stop!
Never stop!
If it rains,
I pray that the rain drops,
reach your skin,
seep through the heart,
crack through the mind,
and reach you.
One day or another,
The flowers will grow,
and be grateful of the thorns.
You must know,
to never stop.

To my friends, sow the seeds of kindness.

It's funny how some flowers remind you of certain people.
Night blooming cereus –
My father once plucked it for my mother,
on a late night stroll,
and the memory brings a smile to his face,
As if he still has essence of that moment.
Maybe he longed for that kind of happiness again.
Maybe he would do anything to get back to that moment.
Blooming motia in my grandma's ears,
which she wore with immense happiness and pride,
like it was the most precious thing she could own.
A delicate glass crown.
Nargis – it reflects who I've become,
a pure narcissist!

Do I resemble a daffodil?

Fluttering and dancing in the breeze?
Continuous as the stars that shine
and twinkle on the Milky Way,

I never forget the first thorn that pierced through my skin – a red
rose.
It is now a constant reminder for me to know,
what pretty things are capable of,
I aim to become such a pretty thing.

The soreness of memories.

I was raised in the city of wolves
and I lived like a lamb.
Only to realise, a lioness prowls beneath my skin
With crocodiles roaming the city every day
and animals called humans howling in the middle of the night
with traitorous yet treacherous hearts and souls
We don't make houses out of wood, out of hay
We build it, brick by brick
strong and sturdy
to save ourselves what wanders in the city.

The art of wrath.

The word impure defines me,
It has absorbed in my skin like henna on a brides hand
The word flares me up
Forms a lump in my throat
A knot in my chest
Wakes up the most unwanted and temporarily forgotten feelings in
the pit of my stomach.
Then it begins
and no matter how much my imaginary self-caring clones try
there is no taming it.

The art of being perfectly imperfect and purely impure.

With always a frown,
In my mind I wonder
If I want to drown
Always in a hurry
It makes life seem so blurry.
I wander into the forbidden places in my mind.
These places offer me a heavenly death.
Peace, happiness, ecstasy.
But it's all just a fantasy.
I'm not allowed there for long.
I wonder if this direction is wrong.
I run and hide.
And end up in the pretty little sunshine
I stare at the sun with my half-moon shades on
I'm just going to let the warmth embrace me.
Just like the moon, I share the light
and then I sunbathe in the moonlight.

I live to see the moon (and you).

A cold breeze
Touched my soul.
My soul
Embraced it like an old friend.
Oh, how lively it feels to be lovely again.
How lovely it feels to feel lively again.
I hear the birds singing in rhythm.
I want to be like them.
The only thing I want right now is to sing.
To feel
To breathe
I am worthy of breathing.
Breathing the air at dawn makes me pure.
There is peace.
So much peace
I have submitted myself to it.
And I never want to leave this place.

Breeze.

I walk on thin ice
with a heavy heaving heart
agony and anger weaved inside
I told you once
I told you twice
I'll slay and rescind if it comes to a fight.

Survival.

Tell me
how do you have that amazing talent to break a heart
that is already broken?
The broken heart that once looked like several shards of glass
now looks like grains of sand.

My pieces are shattered into million pieces.

Love is like hunger
it has no limits
when it starts to make demands
Self-love or self-possessed
when awoke – they're monsters raised from the dead
It makes you make a list of things
of how you were unfair to yourself
how you lied in an unmade bed
how you dug your own grave
how you clawed at your own face
how you spent countless nights crying on cold marble floors
how you spent endless fights with death standing by the door

Love is like hunger
and I have nothing left to give
It is a bottomless pit
as enigmatic as a crying new-born
aberrantly demanding
It has questions
never heard in this world before
It asks why it hasn't been fed properly ever before
now that it's fed
it needs to know more
why now? Why not when I needed to thrive?
This hunger – that I felt
I had to ask it to choke down
on malevolence, wrath and the idea of love instead
survive a little on delusion
a little on fantasy
a little on make-belief ecstasy

Love –
once pure –
Now tainted with malevolence and wrath
doesn't know what to do
when it sees a person with the same hunger it once bore
 the same yearning
It pours the idea of love mixed with the wrath
It feeds the make-belief ecstasy with the idea of tranquility.
and isn't it the perfect recipe for a heartbreak?

Recipe for a heartbreak

First rain in the city of lights.

Karachi — the city of sinners
the city of winners
the city of wolves — with euphoric glimmer
the city of lambs roasted in aromatic spices
striving in crisis
with the high prices
where the boot of big foot
steps on our throats
with yet another plan of destruction.
Just like my city
I don't let go easily
Just like this city of lights
I have darkness inside
same as the darkness that roams the city
every single night
haunts the dreamers
and the preachers
spreading love in a lifeless city of dimmed lights
city of lights — a mirage, irony
the light — it attracts the moths
that get burned in love
then the marauders come
to loot the dead moths
and take the light
leave the darkness of their hearts behind
they take love and spread abhorrence

the city – my city gives whatever it takes
to remain
to remain
to remain – the city of lights
But as my city welcomes a new weather,
the first rain
it isn't just a soft drizzle
it is relentless and ruthless and unforgiving
like me,
this unforgiving rain has taught me one thing:
self-destruction with no promise of faltering
it arrives as it wills
it bends and breaks and destroys and kills
and when it's gone
we ask for more
ignoring the chaos it caused
oblivious of the pain it inflicted
we ask for more
because we can't get enough
until the streets are flooded
less-privileged are bloodied
we ask for more
until we are drenched
some in rain
some in sweat
others, in an endless bloodshed

First rain in the city of lights.

Why do you see things
to understand them?
Haven't you realised yet?
Some things, or maybe everything,
is beyond understanding.
Or maybe it's the unfathomable
and inexplicable unfolding of the divine.

There is an opening that is beyond thought.

You're laughing at the face of sorrow
the city is watching you
the city asks,
you burn so bright,
did you steal my light?

The city had e n o u g h.

What if I told you?
What lies within
skin and bones
and nothing else but HIM and him
would you believe me if I say?
I've decided to extend my stay
depression was the term I fancied
Long ago I shooed it away
Sadness gleams within
Sin and heaven
symphonies and rain
make me wonder
what is it, that makes the heart go all thunder
feathers or wool
whatever you name
covered are us all
with cloth or skin
deny it if you will
but everything, everything happens in this realm as HE wills.

Kun fayakun.

As I stood
in the water
with my feet soaked
I was excited more than the waves
a high tide came
and hit me with all its torrent
When it washed away
I felt my life becoming more
refreshed, happy, and gleaming
and my soul was wiped clean
and I thought,
this is how love ought to be like
where you fall and keep standing at the same time.

Falling.

Don't confuse the light with Noor.
Maybe it's hellfire.
Maybe it's the trick of the devil.
Noor has its purity, the glow and peace within.
No guilt.
No lingering pain.
Noor is Noor.
It can't just be represented by light
It is eternal.
It is ethereal.
Today I saw the sun sink.
But it felt like it will rise right about now.
It felt like Noor is gone.
Lost!
Never to be found again.
I wanted to hold onto the sun.
I felt like,
It will sink so low,
It will forget home,
It will forget me.
How will I see it again?
What will I do without light?
The sun?
what will I do without Noor?

How to find Noor?

And I gifted you a knife for the safety of your own,
but my back constantly hurts,
the reason unknown,
I bleed and ache and bleed some more,
more and more as I crawl down from my throne,
I thought about the time when I was fond of getting stabbed,
and later I found a familiar knife buried in my back.

A lost friend.

I've grown accustomed to whatever pain life may inflict the very next
moment.
I cling to the idea of ungratefulness.
Feeling like filth.
A storm of feelings ricochets through me
every now and then.
But I never completely shed the idea of hope and happiness.

Hoarder of feelings.

I dread being loved
more than I dread being in love.
He wants to give me the world
all I want is a flower.

You are my world.

One second you're breathing.
And in the next one you'll be gone.
Life is a journey of suffering.
Don't make a stop.
Keep moving on.
The journey awaits.
The mountains can't wait.
If you don't budge.
They'll move along.

One second you're regretting.
And in the next one you're forgetting.
Life is a journey, a melancholic song.
Don't stop now.
Your feet have blisters.
The endless road —
Has buried many misters.
You walk on the graves.
Wherever you step.
Be brave! Be brave!
The feet that walks on it,
this is what Earth craves
someone died there
last night where you slept
the warmth Earth gave
Was a cuddle from someone dead
don't sleep!
It's time to weep!
The moment has arrived.
But you didn't thrive
you're in so deep.

One second you're deceiving.
And in the next one you're misleading.
Life is a journey of endless weeping.
Do you want to stop?
Schedule a breakdown?

You can't fly high,
without a little take down.
The wind that touches you.
Has the essence of the past.
Of those who walked on Earth.
The time that existed before time.
The wind is the same.
The one thing, left behind.
The wind will carry you.
It witnessed your stillness.
Why did you stop moving?
Do you have some sort of illness?
Or is it just lack of will?
As if the world is ending.
And you – kept standing.

One second you're cackling.
And on the next one you're clamouring.
Life is a journey of perpetual gambling.
Perch on a branch.
Observe the cyclorama.
Listen to the monotonous melody.
The Earth and the ocean and the song that's sung beneath.
The silver birch, the heath
Ethereal yet real.
Dissolving into the moment like celestial.
The Earth is calling you beneath
To sing you a lullaby
You whispered your secrets to earth
Now it's time to lay inside it
Listen to its cries
The warmth, a hug
The freshness of rain and earth
Fulfilling and somehow divine
Lay my head gently
Absorb me in the gravity
I don't mind being dead, but bruised

Earth, the two story home
First, my mother
Second, my father
the bricks that he jutted together
Painted and decorated and clothed
Now I lay in peace
In the mud bed – without a tent
The lodge with no rent
How long is my stay?
You say it's temporary.
But let's just say
Earth and I – need some time to prate.

The Earthy Melodies.

It's not my fault. I'm high on dreams. It's not my fault.
It's not my fault. I'm high on dreams. It's not my fault.
It's not my fault. I'm high on dreams. It's not my fault.
It's not my fault. I'm high on dreams. It's not my fault.
It's not my fault. I'm high on dreams. It's not my fault.
It's not my fault. I'm high on dreams. It's not my fault.
It's not my fault. I'm high on dreams. It's not my fault.
It's not my fault. I'm high on dreams. It's not my fault.
It's not my fault. I'm high on dreams. It's not my fault.
It's not my fault. I'm high on dreams. It's not my fault.
It's not my fault. I'm high on dreams. It's not my fault.
It's not my fault. I'm high on dreams. It's not my fault.
It's not my fault. I'm high on dreams. It's not my fault.
It's not my fault. I'm high on dreams. It's not my fault.
It's not my fault. I'm high on dreams. It's not my fault.
It's not my fault. I'm high on dreams. It's not my fault.
It's not my fault. I'm high on dreams. It's not my fault.
It's not my fault. I'm high on dreams. It's not my fault.
It's not my fault. I'm high on dreams. It's not my fault.
It's not my fault. I'm high on dreams. It's not my fault.
It's not my fault. I'm high on dreams. It's not my fault.
It's not my fault. I'm high on dreams. It's not my fault.
It's not my fault. I'm high on dreams. It's not my fault.
It's not my fault. I'm high on dreams. It's not my fault.
It's not my fault. I'm high on dreams. It's not my fault.
It's not my fault. I'm high on dreams. It's not my fault.
It's not my fault. I'm high on dreams. It's not my fault.
It's not my fault. I'm high on dreams. It's not my fault.
It's not my fault. I'm high on dreams. It's not my fault.
It's not my fault. I'm high on dreams. It's not my fault.
It's not my fault. I'm high on dreams. It's not my fault.
It's not my fault. I'm high on dreams. It's not my fault.
It's not my fault. I'm high on dreams. It's not my fault.
It's not my fault. I'm high on dreams. It's not my fault.

Mantra for the Dawn

The Cosmic Homecoming

Later did I realise,
You're not Saturn
and I'm not your moon
maybe I'm the lost planet, appeared after millenniums
that came more than close to you
don't confuse me as Titan
because maybe not you, but I am Saturn.

The cosmic homecoming.

I have not lost peace.
I have preserved it.
Covered in raw silk.
In a diamond studded box,
Kept it hidden from the evil eyes.
For the time
when I'm going to need it the most
For now, I love chaos.
And the wounded self
Peace - I know where to go to have it all again.
I know what to do.
I preserve the knowledge.
The pathway to peace
For now, I'll just stay in reality.

Peace of me.

To enter my heart, to break its walls,
there is no need to come with a hammer or swords.
Just come,
With a kind heart, a good word, a warm smile, and pure eyes.
As it already has too much hate in it.
If you bring hate,
You'll be smashed by the walls,
before even thinking about entering.
Sometimes, I have trouble letting people in.
As I have an issue differentiating pleasure and pain.
Not realising, they are actually gifts.
And they have a way of entering my heart.
No matter how tall the walls stand,
they know the way in.

Flooded with fear.

From the person who has been writing endlessly about the moon,
today I'll just say:
Don't be like the moon!
Giving instalments of light with each passing moment
and then one day,
give nothing at all.
Be like the sun!
Give whatever you have.
Give it every day.
Don't be afraid to show up.
Don't be afraid of burning.
Don't be afraid to help the moon shine.
Don't be afraid to bleed into the darkness.
Don't be afraid of the clouds trying to tame your light.
Be the reason owing to which the darkness disappears.
Make darkness afraid of you.
Make the night wait for you.
Be like the sun!
Be like the sun!
Pierce through the darkness.
Reflect the souls.
Make the diamonds shine.
And never rest.
Never sleep.
Never give up.
Stay bright.
Stay shiny.

I live to see the sun.

The sunlight dust flirts with the leaves,
So sublime,
Such serenity.
Flowers open laughing,
And some curl up into themselves.
For the lovers of warmth - it's easy.
But it's the cold that is to fear,
for the life of me – I'll say this isn't fair.

Serenity.

My heart soars at the sight of pink skies
reminds me of the most recent good byes
the sun yawns and drowns itself in the sea
unlike me
the sun has places to be
I witness on my way back home
every dusk, never the dawn
the pink sky bleeds into the blue
and soon it's going to be dark
I must get home
effort requires effort as a friend once said
the success, I heard
comes here with a price
a price of hard work,
of frozen toes I get from walking too much
of pints of coffee and cardamom tea
of hot chocolates to sooth the shivering soul
of candies and sweet cold drinks
and whatever my heart can endure
here, you need a skin for every day
for me, two would do the work
the one I wash off with bleach and wear every day
before stepping out into the world
and let them see what hell I can bring down
I want to be a force to be reckoned with
and the other one, I keep under the bed
the one I brought from home
smells like my mother, kindness and love
I change into it the first chance I get
It heals whatever pain the first one caused.
I didn't come here to grow old
I came here to die young, living
Let's see how that turns out
The one thing I want to do for myself
 is to grow a garden
filled with wildflowers of every colour

so at least my eyes would be able to see the colours
that my soul could never relish
I would sit in this garden
stare at the pink skies longingly
think about the things I have achieved
the person I have become
was it all worth it?
I hope I think that it does.

Pink skies of London.

I'm made of bits and pieces
I fall apart
and I am whole again.

You push me.
Break me
Shatter me
Step on me to move forward.
Lean on me and leave dents on me.
Hold me tight only to bruise me.
Squeeze my heart put salts and spices on my bruised and bleeding
ego.
Choke me to make me swallow my pride.
And I do, I swallow my pride and watch you rise as you walk away.
Just because

I'm made of bits and pieces
I fall apart
and I am whole again.

You take a piece of me to make yourself stronger.
You take my peace to make yourself peaceful.
But not only has it left me weak, it leaves YOU – wilting.
I wait for the sunlight and water.
So, I can grow my missing pieces again.
The bits of sand combine
There is something magical.
And it makes me whole again.
The holes in my heart and head
Flashes light on your wilted souls
My mind hallucinates you to make me see that you are blooming.
And then you see where the light is coming from
And fill those holes with void.
Because breaking and taking my pieces wasn't just enough for you
So, with the void inside my heart
I fail to see your reality.
And then again, you come back.
Because you see that

I am still alive
So, you break me and carve me as you carve a mine for gold.
All you find, is kimberlite.
And you take.
Take and you take.

But how oblivious you are.
Because you have no idea

I'm made of bits and pieces
I fall apart
and I am whole again.

I fall apart.
I wilt, I die.
I grow, I bloom.
And I am whole again.

Take that!

You ask, "Have you ever fallen in love?"
I fall in love every day.
When the sky changes colours.
From blue to grey to pink to violet to black and then blue again
leaving clues as it goes.
I fall in love,
when the first leaf of autumn falls and touches the ground
and the autumn breeze follows me home.
When I see the crimson brown colour of a leaf.
I fell in love,
the first time I saw a sunflower.
And I fell in love,
when I dreamt of dreaming in the lavender fields.

I may be a fantasy, not a reality.

If I realised it before,
How quickly one is shovelled into the Earth,
And into the past,
After their demise.
I never would've wished death upon myself that much.
I'm wrapping the rattling death bell into cotton.
And putting it into a casket.
I'll take it out when the time comes.
It took me the deaths of four loved ones
and frequent self-loathing
to realise that.

Shovelled.

So, bring me a vanilla frosting cake
and flowers that never wither and wilt.
And ask me to stay;
I need reassurance every now and then.
Or maybe every day.
Cling to me!
I'm stitching memory
of how your eyes look like.
When you look at me.

Never stop.

I was down.
Down and dreadful
You were high.
High and colourful
You gave me all of you.
To show me I mean all to you.
You poured your colours into my soul, drop by drop.
Till you had nothing left at all
Then you gave me your wings to see me fly
To see me bright, radiant, and high
How much I am proud to confess.
That you found beauty in my mess
How much I am proud to say.
How we fell in love in just a day
Now when you are left all blue,
I want to sprinkle my colours and share my wings with you!
One for me and one for you
We share our colours every day.
When life decides to rain on our parade
You become green when I am grey.
I become red when I want you to stay.
I turn white to wash your pain away.
You become black to take my darkness away.
You become blue when I turn violet.
Then, we become yellow to ignite our light.
When we reflect in an ocean, there are no words left to say.
We look like Van Gogh's starry night, on a bright and shiny day.

The art of loving.

You laughed when you saw me sinning.
I hope you cry when you see me repent.
The peace that I now have —
I've gone through years of war.
With nafs
to find it.

War.

My heart makes its own decisions.
I lost control over it.
It's not really my fault,
that it chose its home
in you.

You're home, my heart.

Happiness is surrounded by fire.
Protected as it should be.
It is as fragile as a new-born bird.
It is not only for those who are worth it, deserve it or crave it.
It is for everyone!
It is for me.
It is for you.
Hide it when you find it.
Make it the heart's emblem.
Use it to declare peace.

The heart is big enough for both sadness and happiness.

I'll hold up a candle in the middle of a storm.
Useless as it may be.
So, you can find your way back home.
I'll be your lighthouse.
If I must,
then I may
I'll burn myself
like a moth to a flame,
because for you, I want to be the light.

I hope you find yourself in me.

Last night and the night before
the storm tried to barge through my door
It thrashed through my window
But I gave it my thanks
As I desperately needed the sound
that the thunder made
because I wanted to howl and scream
all my heart ache
It muffled the sound of my agonies
and after exhaling all the breath I had
and drying my eyes out till they felt like sand
I felt home
I felt so much at home
In the puddle of tears
entangled with futuristic fears
and the screaming winds
and at that moment I thought
blessed are those
who can feel the pain
blessed are those
who feel like clawing their heart out of their chest
blessed are those
who take a deep breath
and hope for a better tomorrow
Instead of deciding it would be their last breath

Tainted Love.

Only his love can fill this void.
Being with him is like a dream come true.
If I describe him, you won't believe.
He has what it takes to love me.
To help me survive.
I am a flower with poisoned thorns
and he loves me the way I am.
Holds me still.
Piercing himself,
Bleeding.
He holds me still – until,
Life is not a blur anymore.
I can see the light with him.

Too good to be true.

Like a lover's whisper at nigh Like a moth-
er's caress to her child Like the moon calm-
ing the sun down
Like the palette of Van Gogh when paint-
ing the Starry Night. Like the ink and quill
of Shakespeare writing Midsummer
Night's Dream
Like dew drops under the moonlight Like
Virginia Woolf tolerating her own heart
Like me, dreading the New Year to start.)
Like the feeling that
I'd miss the last rain
Like the endless caverns of rain.
Like the notes for the eyes
that shine when the ra
passes
Like how the blood starts to sh
and my heart beats frantically
Like the way you smile when you look at
me This is how love blooms in me

How the love blooms within

There is a secret chord playing in my mind. A fragrant flower I
keep by my side,
A traitorous friend I acclaimed once more.
A treacherous lover who treasures my heart the most
A dew drop on a leaf, living with a heart at free. My happy self
is a ghost of me.
A beautiful secret I tell my eyes.. A symphonious pattern
notes follow. A serene sky with oranges and blues, leading my
heart to follow its shadow
The poignant tune
the telltale of a frail
Illuminating tales that once have fallen me to tale.
Like love of Greek Gods,
but the one to hast to the moors.
In moments there is nothing left to do. The scope of imagina-
tion
is the only thing that lasts forever;
it is the only thing my heart can ever endeavour.

A Symphonized dream.

Like the varying shade of lilac
So certain
So pristine
Dallying with the dreams
Your heart never rests
You're the ocean
The sun willingly drowns in
And as the moon - enchanting
The waves yearn to meet you with whispered sighs
Just like the waves - with their liquid grace
I yearn for your celestial embrace
You pierced through every rag and blanket
I wrapped up around my heart
To keep the cold at bay
Yet you needled your way in
And stitched yourself in with a violet thread
Now everything I say or do is laced with that colour
You dispelled the glooms
With your periwinkle smiles
Your warmth brought fourth
A lilac embrace
You draped me in your kindness
Like a fragile bird drifting in snow
The aura you radiate
Has got me sprinting towards life
No more ideation to darkness as of late
Your life somehow got weaved into mine
With you here, I can now see a better life.

Happy

Like an oyster in the ocean
I wait, patiently
to be filled with something as diminutive as a drop of water
something as little as this
something that has no value in this suffering era of the human world
I wait, for this drop of water
to become something worthy
something as important
as a pearl
to have purity, loyalty, clarity.

Drop of water.

Homesickness – the only disease that bothered to stick with
me
Even when most the diseases found me contagious
and decided to leave me be
This sickness made a home in my heart
No matter where I go
my homeland, my mother, or you
it follows.
what's the cure?
How do I scratch that itch?
I decided to have a séance
and to speak to someone who might know
a little girl with shabby hair
with bright sad eyes made a show
I asked her what the cure to homesickness might be.
She passed me a chalice
and asked me to see
What I saw shook me
for I could never have thought - the little girl smirked
like she was in some secret all along
Stared at myself in the chalice
and the resemblance to the girl was uncanny
How was I to know, I had a home in me.

Home.

Love, love and love alone
 there is nothing else that I have ever known
 Everyone and everything left me to atone
 but love, love, it never let me go
What I did
 What you could never condone
 The only olive branch I was ever extended
 Were my lashes for my tears to hold on
And when we're gone
 they will sing the song of us
 the love and loss and everything within
The things I loved
 the things I lost
There are things, I dare not speak of.

and even after centuries
 this ballad they will come singin'
 remembering the days of the love and loss I endured

When I knock at your door
 I am leaning against it
 I have lost everything but purpose
 answer the call – let me in
It was the true love's kiss that killed me
 it was the true love – the death of me
 your love intoxicated me
I can't live without it now

My eyes beg me not to fall asleep
live, live a little more
little more than everyone else
for you were created for more

My lamenting goes unaccounted for
You are the one at fault
Your love left me in cinders
Come and collect the ashes
If my heart was an ocean
you would see – when you dive in
do it without any qualms
that only one drop holds peace
the rest is just fears,
I am a mariner
I will never lead you astray
my phantom hands would always be there
steering your ship – Only I know it's destiny
Lone, alone and loneliness I have known
Loneliness befell
I know loneliness like love knows me best
I am living the curse over and over
and my punishment is that I can never die

I need a blissful sleep sent from heaven
that can take over my soul
Love never feared to show me
what the mirror failed to
And when we're gone
they will sing the song of us
the love and loss and everything within
"you are a gold mine, hidden in earth, to purify you, we must
set you on fire." – Rumi

The Ballad of What I Could Not Have

Hope takes gratefulness by the hand
Drags it through the meadow of optimism.
It sounds like a sweet dream of a sad life.
Like honey for a sore throat.
Like alimony for a lonely wife.
Hope grabs me by the throat and asks me to take a deep breath.
It asks me to walk on water without thinking of drowning –
Like the water I trusted as a child to carry my paper ships.
It's a wonder how I've seen hope rise and fall.
It's curious, yet dangerous.
How hope makes me want to believe in hope.
How hope allows me to bring people back to life.
How hope tells me, it will all be alright.
I despise honey – too sweet.
I defy hope – too deceptive.
Too much honey can kill.
Too much hope kills more swiftly.
But what if
The cure for the sore throat is honey.
And for the sore heart – is hope.
And what if
the things I defy and despise the most
are my only hopes?

Hope is a dangerous thing for a woman like me.

Lana Del Rey

It's not like I'm going to stay here forever.
I'm a traveller,
just like the others.
We feed off the mother earth.
We sabotage!
And bury ourselves in it.
It is The Ever Welcoming Inn.
Where the memories live,
not us.
They become flesh.
They linger,
and they sting.
The 5:00 am morning breeze,
carries my memories.
Confesses my love for that time
and passes it on
to the other travellers.
And making them the new observers
of the world around,
of the breaking of dawn,
of the beauty and life.
And everything that goes around,
always finds its way to come around.

Secret whispers of the wind.

I stopped talking to the mirror,
since it started talking back.

You ought to hear the mirror in my house!

there is hope. there is light. there is hope. there is light. there is hope.
there is light. there is hope. there is light. there is hope. there is light.
there is hope. there is light. there is hope. there is light. there is hope.
there is light. there is hope. there is light. there is hope. there is light.
there is hope. there is light. there is hope. there is light. there is hope.
there is light. there is hope. there is light. there is hope. there is light.
there is hope. there is light. there is hope. there is light. there is hope.
there is light. there is hope. there is light. there is hope. there is light.
there is hope. there is light. there is hope. there is light. there is hope.
there is light. there is hope. there is light. there is hope. there is light.
there is hope. there is light. there is hope. there is light. there is hope.
there is light. there is hope. there is light. there is hope. there is light.
there is hope. there is light. there is hope. there is light. there is hope.
there is light. there is hope. there is light. there is hope. there is light.
there is hope. there is light. there is hope. there is light. there is hope.
there is light. there is hope. there is light. there is hope. there is light.
there is hope. there is light. there is hope. there is light. there is hope.
there is light. there is hope. there is light. there is hope. there is light.
there is hope. there is light. there is hope. there is light. there is hope.
there is light. there is hope. there is light. there is hope. there is light.
there is hope. there is light. there is hope. there is light. there is hope.
there is light. there is hope. there is light. there is hope. there is light.
there is hope. there is light. there is hope. there is light. there is hope.
there is light. there is hope. there is light. there is hope. there is light.
there is hope. there is light. there is hope. there is light. there is hope.
there is light. there is hope. there is light. there is hope. there is light.
there is hope. there is light. there is hope. there is light. there is hope.
there is light. there is hope. there is light. there is hope. there is light.
there is hope. there is light. there is hope. there is light. there is hope.
there is light. there is hope. there is light. there is hope. there is light.

Mantra for the midnights

سب کچھ اختتام پذیر ہے

Everything comes to an end

"This is how it always is when I finish a poem,
a great silence overcomes me
and I wonder why I ever thought to use language."
Rumi, a Thirsty Fish

"And as to me, I know nothing else but miracles". -
Walt Whitman, Leaves of Grass

"I am the daughter of Earth and Water,
And the nursling of the Sky;
I pass through the pores of the ocean and shores; I
change, but I cannot die."
Percy Bysshe Shelley, The Cloud

Dictionary

His/Him - Allah
Noor - Pure light
Ammi - Grandmother
his/him - Love of my life
motia - Jasmine
Abbu - Grandfather
Chasing cars - A song by snow patrol
Habits - A song by Plested
Finch - Character from All the bright places by Jennifer Niven
Cereus - a flower that symbolizes false hopes for the people living,
being drawn to it represents readiness to face the fears
Nargis - Daffodil
Sukoon - Peace
Karachi - My city
Kun fayakun - Be, and it is.
Malefic - Destructive, Harmful
Nafs - Self or soul

Author's note

I wish, like those before me, that my tears can be translated into words.

About the Book

From the catacombs of memory, I wrote these testaments of pain to describe my ruined pride. I have dived into the cobwebs of suppressed memories to concoct this poetry and had fitful episodes of sleep when I tried to reach for each trivial part of me. A faint whisper calls me as I fall into the pitfalls of fantasies. During this process, the darkness swallowed me whole, and I obliged. I weaved in some happy moments and rose from the depths of despair. I became a wolf in lambs clothing, ready to scavenge with words laced with pure venom instead of claws. There's poetry brewed in this book. The smell I find so delightful. Broken words and sighs knit together to make this poetry worthwhile. But the suffering of this city, the noose of death, and its unbearable stench grew tighter around my neck every time I took a breath and wrote.

About the Poet

A 29-year-old and ever aging, high-spirited soul currently calling Kent, England home, though my roots trace back to Karachi, Pakistan. With enthusiasm and a penchant for deep emotions, I find solace and joy in writing. Poetry is my refuge, it's the best feeling in the world to moonlight as a poet every single night. My love for poetry extends to the profound words of Jalal-ud-din Rumi, Walt Whitman and Sylvia Plath, while Elif Shafak, Charlotte Bronte, Jane Austen and Paolo Coelho hold special places in my heart as my favourite authors.

Acknowledgements

From the quietest and loudest corners of my heart, I find the words to thank those who have shaped my life and this book. No one writes alone, even if the act itself feels solitary. Every page carries the presence of the people who helped me endure, reflect, and continue.

To my parents, thank you for bringing me into this world and allowing me to experience the inexorable multitude of feelings that eventually found their way into these pages. Your love, care, and protection have been the quiet foundation beneath my life and my writing. I may never fully understand the depth of the sacrifices you made for me, but I carry immense gratitude for everything you have given me, both seen and unseen. Without your presence and guidance, I would not have had the courage to feel so deeply or to write so honestly.

Shadman, my husband, the love of my life, you kept resuscitating me even when I thought there was no use. You are and always will be the love of my life. I would go under the mountain for you, though you have no clue what I mean by this. You held my spine together (a book doesn't exist without a spine) with a strength I could not always find within myself and encouraged me to keep moving forward when standing still felt easier. This book, and perhaps even the person who wrote it, would not exist without you.

To Ali and Beenish, my siblings who have been beaten by life time and time again yet never lost their strength. You always stood back up and carried on. Your resilience gives me strength in ways I cannot fully ex- plain, and through my wonderful nieces and nephews you remind me that joy continues to grow even in difficult times. I truly love the family that I have and would never trade you for any other.

To Saviya, the sun to my sunflower, the Shams to my Rumi, the Starry Night to my Van Gogh. Words feel insufficient when I try to describe what your presence in this journey has meant to me. As the editor of this book, you did far more than simply refine words on a page. You walked beside me through every poem, every hesitation, and every moment of doubt.

You read every line with care, questioned what needed questioning, and helped polish what needed patience. Many of the quiet strengths within these pages exist because you helped me see them more clearly.

Thank you for staying up late with me despite the distance and the time zones between our countries, for reading every poem and looking through every illustration with me. Our countless late night conversa- tions about poetry, life, and meaning have shaped this book in ways that may remain invisible to the reader but will never be forgotten by me. Your intellect, honesty, and devotion to this work have strengthened it beyond measure. Your love has kept me alive and moving forward through years that often felt unbearably heavy. I will forever repay this gratitude in cups of coffee, books, and chocolates. You are happiness given form and the colour yellow.

To Hira, you forced this book into existence, thank you for standing beside me through moments when words felt too heavy to carry alone. Your presence has been a quiet reassurance in my life, a reminder that kindness and understanding still exist in a restless world. You have lis- tened patiently, offered comfort when I needed it most, and supported me with a sincerity that I deeply value. Your encouragement, whether spoken in long conversations or in simple moments of reassurance, has helped me continue when the path ahead felt uncertain. For your friend- ship, your patience, and your steady belief in me, I am truly grateful.

Fariha, thank you for your unwavering support, love, and encourage-
ment. You have been both my rock and my refuge throughout this
jour- ney. More than anyone, you have lived inside these pages with
me as the main beta reader of this book. You patiently read through
my poems again and again, offering thoughtful reflections, careful
feedback, and encouragement whenever doubt began to grow too
loud. Your deep love for books and literature inspires me every day.
The way you cherish sto- ries and words constantly reminds me why
writing matters. Your enthu- siasm breathed life back into me when I
feared my voice might fade. Be- cause of you, these poems became
braver than I ever expected them to
be.

To Hira Naz, my first true friend who has seen everything, perhaps
far too much, and still never let me go. You never gave up on me even
when I had nearly given up on myself. Your presence has been a quiet
anchor through many storms in my life.

Mawra, your faith in me has never wavered even once since the day I
came to know you. That quiet certainty you hold in me has been a
rare and beautiful gift. Thank you for believing in me so effortlessly
and so completely. I love you for that more than words can properly
express.

And to Ayesha, who began helping me without even realising it and
who has kept me alive for years with her simple messages every morn-
ing saying good morning and have a good day. There is a purity in
your kind- ness that reminds me that even the smallest gestures can
carry profound meaning. Thank you. You mean more to me than you
know.

Sidra, you have seen me completely and still call me an inspiration.
Your belief in me has given my words the courage to exist.To my beta
readers Akanksha, Arbish, and Fariha, thank you for your in- valu-
able insights and thoughtful feedback.

Your time and care helped shape these poems into what they are today. To Arbish, thank you for reading these poems with care and for your thoughtful feedback and en- couragement. To Akanksha, thank you for your insights and for taking the time to engage so thoughtfully with these poems.

Writing poetry is often a solitary endeavour, but it is the people in my life who make it meaningful. Nature, with its seasons and mysteries, has long been my muse. Libraries and bookstores have offered me shelter when I sought refuge in the written word and the artistry of those who came before me. The stars and the moon have whispered quietly in dark- ness, revealing fragments of truth that eventually found their way into these pages.

This book stands as a testament to the many hands, hearts, and sourc- es of inspiration that have touched my life.

And to you, dear reader, for picking up this book. These poems are a piece of my soul. In sharing them, I hope they find resonance within your own experiences, feelings, and dreams.

Lastly, I offer my deepest gratitude to the poets of the past whose words have accompanied me throughout this journey. You are the shoulders upon which I stand while gazing toward the horizon of in- spiration.

9 781535 606509